PRAISE for the poetry of Nate Pritts

"Pritts's world is rich, vivid, intimate, and somewhat troubled."

Justin Taylor in *Poetry*

"The flights and whims of Pritts's imagination hit hardest when he creates a form inside which they can ricochet. [...] In these moments, the poems [...] arrive at a place of vulnerability and sincerity."

Publishers Weekly

"At a time when poetry that favors exuberance is approached with timidity, Nate Pritts attacks, with colloquial speech, our preconceptions of whether a poem can, in fact, be devoted to wonder and pleasure."

Curtis Perdue in *Redivider*

"The velocity of Pritts's verse is unusually ecstatic— ecstatic but not frantic. In addition to his adept ability to surprise with double meanings that often occur through enjambment, his control is apparent in the stanza breaks and the attention paid to the individual line as a single, self-embodied unit."

Jake Levine in *HTMLGiant*

"The only person more dangerous than a dark-hearted man is a dark-hearted man on a sunny day."

Melissa Broder in *The Rumpus*

RIGHT NOW MORE
THAN EVER

RIGHT NOW MORE THAN EVER

Nate Pritts

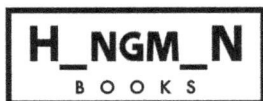

H_NGM_N
B O O K S

www.h-ngm-nbks.com

For a complete listing of titles, or for more on this book, visit:

www.h-ngm-nbks.com
www.h-ngm-n.com/right-now

TABLE OF CONTENTS

Who would have thought that I'd be here, nothing
    wrapped up, nothing buried, everything
Love, children, hundreds of them, money, marriage-
    ethics, a politics of grace,
Up in the air, swirling, burning even or still, now
    more than ever before?

Ted Berrigan

RIGHT NOW MORE
THAN EVER

DEMONSTRATED MELANCHOLY

I would like to request a volunteer.
Please raise your hand

only if you are a lovely singer
in possession of your own voice.

Please raise your hand only if your hand
is actually a sunflower. Some materials

will be supplied but others
you should bring from home. You must

have a home from which you can bring things.
I need help reconstructing these crayons

that broke in half after she told me
what I kept drawing wasn't right enough.

I have a thing for dinosaurs & lunar cities.
I was trapped in a mythical past; I was imagining

an improbable future.
I need you to bring me a really long saw because

I am going to put you in this box
& prove that I understand the finality

of separation. You're going to need
to bring some replacement parts

for the parts of you damaged in the performance.
I'm going to cover you with a sheet

& when you disappear you will need to yell
indicating to the congregation

that you are disappearing. Can you yell
frantically? I may need to say "I am in love with you"

but trust me: it's only temporary. When I snap
my fingers, you'll wake up & forget all of this.

TALKING ABOUT AUTUMN RAIN

I hereby submit this yellow leaf as my charter,
wet & preserved under snowpack – Syracuse
blunt, a backyard bluster of stark white –

though it's early December which means it's
autumn & the rains that rain & melt the snow
are still autumn rains. Sirs: This application contains

six parts – a missing casement, two atria, two
vehicles & respected sobbings. Also,
more than a gallon of blood. Please wear gloves

when handling to ensure proper emotional distance
from the exploding world I can't make sense
of. Enclosed, please find a suspension bridge

of glued popsicle sticks & a rough sketch
of a mechanical calla lily that blooms on demand,
complete with conveyor belt attachment to deliver

that quiet beauty anywhere in the compartmental
soul overnight. We can all wake up to love. Also
random gears. Also teeth. Items listed may have

settled during shipping. People may have learned
to accept the same pale things they railed against

in the bright sunshine of their morning lives.

I'm certain where I'm going is cold. In preparation
I've scooped out my own brain & ziplocked it
for freshness, I've plucked my eyeballs out, one by

one by one, & dropped them into clay jars next to
the heart-shaped shard framed on the wall.
My messterpiece. My late blue period. I'll call it

Faith because I won't need my senses in this new world.
I'm decapitating myself to see everything brand new
& thanks in advance for your consideration. I hope

you'll incorporate this bewilderment, solidify this relentless
uncertainty. I sign my papers with an X between trees
signifying where to dig, ignoring a road sign saying turn back.

Make this organization sing.

ENGAGEMENT PROTOCOL

Life is but a trigger   so what happens
happens in the roots
        or it happens in the air
air that's empty when you look
but is positively charged when you try
to recall it. Sometimes the horizon
is so complicated because perspective
is a trick we play on ourselves.
You put your mouth to the fire
        or your mouth is the fire
you amplify every moment
        make it colossal
        make it exactly as small as it really is
& what happens next is just bedtime
then nightmares a drive mostly east
back to the place where I stand
a place I know I should better defend.
There are so many days I only talk
at myself.   I don't say a single real word
to anyone else. No one questions
what no one can hear   & I whisper
every good & bad thing in such fragile
weather grey rainy cold
        then record highs
the complex atmosphere between all of us
how much love there is

       how much dis / connection
passion & loss. Standing outside
with a beer & already I'm feeling everything
collapse into one vital body.
If we're lucky it never dies   even
when it exhausts itself   even when
it expires. Friendship & loneliness
are my two favorite colors.

THE HILLS HAVE JUSTICE

Sunflowers on the kitchen table,
on the bathroom counter, sunflowers
hanging in the closet waiting to be worn
then swallowed whole to make my voice
the brightest new light in a field
of lightheadedness. Above it all,
the sky full of stars though it's 1:30 pm.
We can be forgiven for not noticing
the burn.   When I don't notice something,
I do it strong. I keep my eyes fixed
on the wall, on the ridiculous head
of the sunflower reflected in the mirror
instead of the real one in real life where it matters.
I will never confess what I did.
I will never reflect on my life
so I won't have to feel bad about it.
Overhead, the sky full of etcetera
etcetera, full of verse chorus verse.
My heart a vacuum in June. My head
full of bad dreams, hundreds of them
every night like sharp stars.
The lake full of monster.
Every city has one, something big
under the surface waiting to destroy it
before some other beast gets the pleasure.

My new name is City, my address
unreadable. The traction
that I feel is what holds me in place –
not morals, not gravity, not the Foundation
or the Academy. I've been a rebel
my entire life. I'm waiting for the pain
to set like a sun. Then we'll all see
the things that are there to be seen.
The birds in my chest where my heart should be.
The hills full of Justice. This fall,
every leaf will turn its own type of golden,
voices together as they fall in the fall.

GHOST OFFICER

My head gets shoved deep into the machine.
I come home to a letter from the servants
demanding the very last whisper

you left in my ear; they want to take anything
I don't want them to. Some August leaves
still in the mailbox, right next to the bills.

Those leaves were once open, gasping
like a palm. Like September had started,
all that red with only a breath of yellow.

They can't believe they're not what they were.

COLLECTED RECOLLECTIONS

There was the time that wooden chair had
a banana peel on it, bright yellow & shining.

There was the time there was no wooden chair
nor banana peel, or the wooden thing was me

& there was something shining or not
shining at all. Sailboats drift in a harbor

or in other wet environments. Also no sailboats,
not drifting. Fifteen different kisses you remember.

Three different people & the long division. Kissing
things, things kissing. There was the moon.

There was a new moon & there was no moon.
I was dressed like the leading man in a romantic comedy

from the 1940s, debonair in grey flannel. A flower
in my hand or a flower in my hand held out to you.

I was dressed like the leading man in a Romantic poem
from the 1840s, soaking wet in ruffles. O I fall

upon the thorns of life several times per season
but most often in the Spring. It could have been any day

in the whole wonderfull yeare. There was
the time I said something profoundly affecting

in emotional & intellectual ways. I had blue eyes
when I said what I said. I know because you

told me. I wanted to say the sky was the sky
whether there were birds cluttering it or not.

THERE HAS ALWAYS BEEN
A GREAT DARKNESS

Orphaned cars line the streets.
They all start wondering

about the lineage of their upholstery.
Questions repeated without variation

make the congregation uncomfortable
in their hats. Without warning

they're reminded that they have hair
yelping to be set free! Say one thing

over & over into the atmosphere
& you'll convince the stars to believe it.

Or else they'll decide that they're dead
already. Welcome to summer, the aroma

of a freshly chopped backyard. Sometimes,
we need a red blink to remind us it's dangerous

to cross from one life to the next.
It reminds us to wake up. On Tuesdays,

the green blooms into a comet & we forget

to hate the barriers that entrap us.

Such a beautiful orange trumpet!
Sometimes a keyhole is shaped like a cloud.

Those same words escaped me three times
because I wanted their sincerity

to sway people to have faith in me.
It was something I did to stave off the darkness.

ORIGAMI BIRD IN OCTOBER
MONDAY LIGHT

My car in late autumn cold. My chest
full of foggy breaths. The whispered
hush of me drifting out. I say bird
& it is a kind of bursting from the tree
I saw yesterday that I still need to tell you about.
Even one hundred people can agree
about the feathers & the colors but not
the tree that I haven't yet said much about.
Remember last winter & paper snowflakes
in the windows. Remember snowflakes
not melting in the sunshine. The Mondayness
of this light. I still get distracted by clouds;
almost two weeks now & my morning eyes
are stifled by cloud in this present Octoberousness.
There are things that only happen once
happening all the time! Someone held a bird
& said to me "For you." Someone made a bird
out of paper so it wouldn't disappear in the heat.
I'm writing every poem to you. When I run
in the distant cold of this season, my chest hurts.
I'm writing every one of these poems to me.
There was a tree. There was a break in the trees
& I saw a tree & there was one less leaf in me.
My eyes were cold & cloudy. There was a tree
& it was full of leaves or full of the places leaves

had recently been & I could still see the colors.
Remember a black wire table in the mountains
in my chest. Remember trying to cry. Remember
hundreds of paper hearts, O golden in the sunset!
There was a tree yesterday that might have held
thousands of leaves or snowflakes or tears or birds,
or thousands of years of trying to be better.

SENTIMENTAL SPECTACULAR

Of all the snowflakes rocketing early
through the late fall air, I'm only going to remember

the forty or so stuck to your hair.
Darling, darling, darling,

there's something sensational in the way
my heart takes on different forms

according to the temperature, something
spectacular about holding your hand

on a planet we share as it keeps turning & turning.
Or instead it's early fall & curled yellow leaves

line the sidewalks of a city we don't live in
& I'm kicking them up & shouting yay!

Imagine strobe light attention on anything
that brings a smile to your face; imagine

a balloon drifting over the lake carrying
a message about who to contact if the note

is found. Such big bright hope drifting.
I'm writing words again, unsure who'll

read them or if anyone will read them.
I'm writing complex math equations

on slips of paper & distributing them
to an audience of people who can't read

math equations: $1 + 1 =$ morning is when
I am awake & there is a dawn in me &

blue sky $+$ impending rain $=$ I love you.
My only response is to kiss you; no matter what

is happening, it's happening. I'd like to throw
a party, I'd like to toss it up into the sky

& watch it float & I'll let it fall down
when I'm ready. I'll give you this me

to keep, your very own me forever & ever,
because it's what we both deserve.

TULIP STREET

People are acting crazy in February
because their lives are nothing

but marks & lines. They are inexplicable
to themselves. They are their own ending,

one that resonates, that multiplies possibility
instead of zeroing out. Walking around,

there is the juxtaposition of a nine foot snow drift
with something like the sun & blue sky

& rising temperature. Maybe it's okay
to be showing your arms. The sunlight

is racing up & down the bare branches of these trees
that are trying to be stoic when instead the wind

is having its way with them & I'm pretty convinced
I've forgotten how to write a poem which is what

I've been trying to do the last few months.
Forgetting, I mean. Then suddenly the dramatic

& loving curve of a leg outlined in blue jean
is staring me directly in the eye & I'm out of breath

even thinking about it. Also I've forgotten
how to write a sentence & I don't care about the poetic

utterance so I just make sure that what I'm saying
is what I'm thinking all at once. I notice

the snow melt & how there is just some green
exposed in the park which reminds me & everyone

about spring. Not today, but it'll happen soon
for real, the real will be real & the flowers

we see will be mad with movement,
loud colors in the world instead of memories.

FROST AT MIDMORNING

This is year one, right now, & there's
news of the world coming across the wire,
news on the march, or it's March
& it's really October & time ravages on
or it's Syracuse & I'm waking up lonely
with arms that can't do what they know to do,
palms shaped like empty rosebuds.
Someone wearing the stilly hush
of nature hands me an updated report
or I'm the report he gives me, I'm a gun
going off, I'm bang: frost weighs down
the leaves cluttering the ground, rainbow
patchwork puzzle that doesn't form
anything other than what it is. Frost
& red leaves, frost on the car, secret ministry
of frost on each of my lonely fingers
so they can't bend; they snap. The velocity
of this velocity careening through the thicket.
What about the gentle breathings of bodies
smashing into lakes? There's a line thin
as a lute string between romance & one hundred
possible deaths in each sunset we circle
as the big bright sun circles us, orbiting
all of this in a blind reverie haze determined
to gather the necessary information

to send back to base. Me a proud honorary
astronaut sent out as a lover of uncontained
& immortal beauty but, O, just a chump in love
with the ground, the feet of the real buried
in sand on a beach you can't reach except
in memory. Frost in autumn, frost at midnight,
Frost on a hotel bed, telescoping from mountains
to buzzsaws, each of your eyes a diamond
ripping through my wooden soul, a stunning
revelation no matter which of five mountain ranges
you're planted on & I am wildly annunciatory;
I am some pine tree utterance; I am a broken
sonnet shattered in the fall & fitted back together.
I'm a poem written on the back of a faded map
to your house. How simple the cavernous twists
& turns when we can see the ways we'll move in advance
of the broken life. I woke up from a dream of frost
covered leaves to a world of frost covered leaves.
I brooded all the following morn. I listened to my heart.

ASSEMBLY DIRECTIONS

We watched the clouds moving
& were really impressed.

It's what was called for so that's what happened.
After a walk, after some water.

When I wanted to lay down
you made me some trees & my shoulders

rebelled so you told them to rest.
I couldn't begin to name the parts

that make this what it is.
It's because in the morning

your body stretches across me
& I can't see myself without seeing you too.

It's because of some danger.
It's because of this living.

Then another day with no power,
the people silent though their nature was deep,

truly truly emphatic. The two of us talking,

the sun always setting.

Then the rain started in just so it could stop.
Then we went walking. See yourself

in the mirror & notice the light,
the light that's much brighter & suddenly full.

If you spread out the pieces & follow
directions, you might finish the day

with a new place to stand.

IN MEMORY OF MY FEELINGS

Even gentle breezes fracture
this blue sky, these silver clouds

cracked & sparkly pink, stunned
spinning air that shakes loose

the stupefied & last leaves of this
sentimental season, a spectacular

racket of branch & bird to blast
the dust off this October quietness

& this private me, this public me,
this me transparent to myself.

One of me is driving his car
down the grey road of this Syracuse

& one of me is just watching
a rain of red & orange in a photo.

One of me runs
all morning blanketed in sun, coated

in chill & each leaf smacks each me
in the face suddenly like terror

or hesitantly like love. Or orangely,
a big bright heart resting like

a sun on the horizon, setting us
on a trajectory that makes sense.

There's one of me aimed at bliss,
hellbent on happiness & one of me

circling like a leaf caught in a draft
of wind & one of me keeping pace

with one of you, holding your breath
in his solid hand & holding your hand

in his gusty breath, reading
road signs like they're works of art

with hidden meanings. Storms churn
like a gift at the edge of a painting,

paper ragged like a dream that shouldn't
scare us but does. Today is the best

today I can remember & one of me
burns for you exactly like I burn for you.

LOCOMOTIVE IN AUTUMN

My heart in early scattered sun.
Clouds, O lovely & descending.
This fragmentation.

This constant slow method
expressed. This revelated sunflower.
I spent last night reading a letter

you never wrote me.
I knew every word
& phrased every apology.

Each of the last three days,
I couldn't blink the clouds
from the morning. Now

it's a week later.
I'm putting words on paper.
The poet says *her heart*

like it's a phrase in a song,
like that red damage is singing,
broken & gorgeous. My heart

is a tree. My song is a bird.

Sometimes I am sparrow.
Sometimes I am distant

from myself & sometimes
I am something shinier.
Sometimes the sun sets

& things that shouldn't be
golden are golden. There's a field.
There's a lake & a tree & a bird.

Sometimes I am goldenrod crowding a field.
Leaves fall from my branches
but I try to hold on.

Sometimes I am lost to myself,
breathing the season's departure,
& I can smell the snow.

One cloud, this one bird
& me & you naming everything.
It looks like it could all blow up

so easily. Does this make it better?
Do you believe in rapture?
That something could make you

so happy that you burst
into bursting? Sometimes I am rapture.
Sometimes I am locomotive in autumn

& there's an explosion
deep in my chest to keep me going
on & on steadily over the prairie.

POST FALLOUT LETTER

Read this after. Purple sky reminds me
of lots of purple things including sky.
I might be in this lane or that lane.

The explosions around me might actually
be me or just a lazy puffball dandelion
after a held breath, a wish then blow.

You have to remember how to breathe
when holding an envelope full of leaves;
I'm holding the same exact love in these

lumberjack hands. It could be Tuesday
or not Tuesday; it could be fall or winter.
Constellations are pictures if you pull back

but I'm worried what will happen
if you pull back. Suddenly, thousands
of white dots burning. You'll see I'm not

perfect. You'll see I'm 78 miles per hour,
driving around blue lakes on a glowing map.
You'll want to know which part of the tab

is yours. The question of what you owe,

& to whom, hangs in the purple night, moon
glowing in clouds like the heart of darkness.

Help me get it right. I've made a list
of the things I can't talk about.
I'll hide it somewhere hidden like a bomb.

WHEN MAN DISCOVERED HE COULD
INVISIBLY DELIVER MOVING

My arms felt like arms. My arms felt like arms
or a new category of response to beauty
& the air was invisible with invisible snow

which meant it was like a picture
with the sound turned down, a rush of music
we strained to hear. We were standing in February

on the street between her car & mine
but we stood together & I was falling apart
& she was maybe falling apart & we held each other

like we meant it forever but knew it was just a breath
upon leaving. There was something moving.
There was a clamor in my heart, the distant light

of dead stars. I'm dodging this sentiment with words
to keep from crying out. I am not a Poet
& this is not a Poem. There were ghosts

running through my veins & my eyes woke up
searching the sky for birds that weren't there.
We wanted plummet & burn. I fell

& discovered fire. Now there's nothing

left to burn, dim car hazards blinking
as we kissed in orange strobe.

There were too many kinds of damage.
I discovered I could throw off sparks.
I held it all together & then let it go.

FLAMINGO POEM POEM

I'm going to flamingo this flamingo
into flamingo & call it Poem.

I'm going to golden sun behind clouds,
feather & haze propped up on one supporting

fact like a leg plunged in water. Exuberant
declaration! O Insight, O Epiphany!

I'm going to diction. I'm going to shifting
tone: serious consideration given to the Fanciful

bursting off. I'm going to poem this poem into poem
& call it Flamingo. I'm going to mimetic theory.

One can write a flamingo that calls
attention to itself as flamingo & still make it

flamingo—embed it with flamingos of dawn, rising
& orange, flamingos of starlight, burning

forever, flamingos of the cave, empty & raging.
I'm going to big bright light in the cave

to sweep away those shadows. I'm going to

set the woods on fire: because pledge to beauty

everlasting, because I love you, because
God writes trees & reading is building a house

of the trees God made. So I want you to stand
in the field with me. There is no shelter here.

I wrote a flamingo mimicking the flamingo
of flamingo. Flamingo golden in eternity, feasting

on the trembling Ephemeral; Nate blue & ephemeral,
trembling, no matter how much love you feed him.

INARTICULATE BIRD

Every person I see today
is not you in any way at all.

But I'm ecstatic about it
because why not

blare a horn when nothing
is moving? How many clouds

does it take to block out the sun
when the sun is really a thing

in your heart burning?
Don't forget the promise of mathematics,

the luminous transitive property
which states that if I talk

about beauty & let it stain my lips,
& if you talk about beauty

then I can make your lips mine.
A ramshackle nest we are

destined to drop from.

This poem is only a Poem

so it is not the actual love you want.
You can't kiss it, can't hold it

to your chest & give it a name.

IT WAS JUST THINKING

They each were a glass breaking.
The size of two hummingbirds.

My feelings about the morning.
I was looking at the light

& getting it confused with some other
light. I knew the answer

to every question was written down

somewhere, folded away
so that I could see only that it was there.

I have a picture of a picture of your smile
that I refer to when there isn't enough sun.

On those days I let my heart wallow.
It often collapses. Each shift of the sun

indicates something. I have it programmed
to let me know that time is passing.

RIGHT NOW MORE THAN EVER

RISE TIME

It's too overwhelming
        all the data that's happening
the crash of the instruments

        the stars zeroed out
                O so dead before we get their light.

To be an emergency contact every day of the week
you need to be safe   you need to be calm.

        Leave your phone on
but turn your radio louder.

Real life surrounds us says my friend
        & he's right about that & about everything else.

I heard a surprising sound
        in the living room & I thought the lamp
was broken / was dropped to the floor.
I saw a million pieces of lamp in my head.

I knew then that my life's work would be reassembly
        & I thought that would be a fine way to live.

No more eyes to see with / just an instruction book.

No brain & no heart / only guidelines.
No more reason to fear the void
                    which tries so hard to devour us whole.

No fear.

What can save us? Where do we turn?

Real life is all around us & it's running out.

✳

I'm dazzled by the quality of my friend's deep attention

the way he sees everything
                              the pain & the planets
          the backyard full of toys

the essential & insubstantial   mess of it all

the focus that he chooses which is everything together
              on top or underneath   a collage of sympathies

& both of us are real people.

                    We both have kitchen tables.

Mine is covered with books & some fruit
              a shaker from Bulgaria full of Cambodian black pepper

one hundred napkins just waiting for a mess
              some letters to mail tomorrow when I go to work.

But all of this is stuff that I want to forget
              because I know I will anyway   eventually.

It's my sad quest to divest every moment of meaning

before it runs out on me & leaves me alone.

The dailyness floors me / gives me faith / bankrupts me
& breaks me.

My current position is right here in hiding
trying to pretend I don't even exist.

I reach out my hand through the breeze that's gathering

the wind that means something precious is ending.

✖

I like a wild cosmos

        &I like a little loneliness
because it keeps me honest.

Daily I'm reminded of the danger that surrounds us
as well as that it's okay
        since it's more interesting to risk extinction
than safely never make decisions.

What I love about love is that it's a problem
how you can never take other things into yourself
        enough   or never see yourself reflected

in every mirror all at once.
All you can do is ache   & stay alive.

        Stay open to the hurt of separation
because it's full of possibilities.

This is a Human Universe
        & all the stars are dying.
Reality grounds us / but you can't always trust it.

This is the anthem I kept repeating while I slept.
I was worried I'd forget the words

but my heart is always beating
& even when it stops I'll still be on fire.

I go downstairs   I make the morning coffee
I look out the window & see everything happening.

✴

Dear Matt,   It's Sunday.

I worry a lot about you   getting tired
wearing out & then disappearing
but I realize I'm projecting.
You're a reflector   & the whole world
is sunshine / you point yourself out
while I bury my head   while I run the old filmstrip
one more time again.

                    I'm too much a ruin
because of the past & every word I write
is trying to bring myself at peace with the scatter

We drove to my mom's house   two actual people –
Nate & Jenny   Syracuse New York
          the town that we live in.
I had to stop at the park because I was worried
I'd forget the words to the tune of my life
          that mindless humming
the thrumming of all the possibilities
I only sometimes can recognize. The hazards

are flashing to let the other drivers know
          I'm not moving
that the stars all around are us are ending their light show
          that each of us is dying right where we stand.
The days are endless until they stop.

Human energy brings the monster to life:
art & love   all the things that matter.
You shout the present alive with your mouth.

I see it all turning into a ghost

✖

Real life astounds us
            all the other people & all the other things.

Even when I'm trying it's hard to be specific.
It's easier for me to be vague because I'm scared.

Scared that maybe if I tell everyone what I love
I won't love it anymore   or I'll still love it
            hard
                        & it will disappear anyway.

Once upon a time long long ago
I was born in Syracuse & immediately
                        started dying.

My light was so bright   then it flickered.

RIGHT NOW MORE THAN EVER

WELCOME TO PARADOX

Every clock in the building
has a different idea
about its prime function   about
when we die. This is the daydream
I always wanted   this proliferate meaninglessness
even when I was a kid   trying to race
the shadows of the clouds
           the birds that never seemed content.
Who can sit still   when the option
is flight?   I spend too much time
wondering   how to judge the fall.
I drive home from work to eat my lunch.
           I'm just sending out signals
which report back what's happening around me.
Turns out not much   at least nothing
more than anyone could see
           with undamaged eyes.   Mine
get splotchy in the late afternoon.
The vision gets crowded by strobes of light
& I can't   focus   on the center
which is where everything happens.
I worry every day that I'll go blind
                         though not enough
to really do anything about it.   I'm the man
without fear.   I wish I could stay
on the highway forever   forever & never

stop. My brain gets so loose & makes up so much
unpredictable noise.   At home
the backyard was overrun
          with butterflies
but I cut six wooden stems off the lilac bush
anyway   one for each room in the house.
          I made a big bowl
of guacamole to stave off being anxious.
I didn't use enough lime juice
or   I used so much lime juice
are two different directions this poem
could take.   Both of them are real
& both of them matter.   The poem
is the place where I work out possibilities
instead of in real life where there are consequences
          where the results could be disastrous.
It's a field where everything happens
                    simultaneously & is true
& you believe it all equally
just to see   where it leads. I'm on the highway
screaming in my car. On the table
right here   everything is green
& delicious   because it's real.
Except for the lilacs   which are purple
but also real   & don't taste at all
like what you'd expect.

CALM POEM

It's November 15th. I've never been
Nate Pritts today. Early morning

& already there's a halo of helicopters
harrowing the blue, sending word

through the static about crowded intersections—
all that crosstown traffic. I don't care

if it's calm. Calamity is okay.
Early morning & the buzz is circling

my head like a certainty.
Three or four times a day,

I feel like I'm about to get shot out of myself,
like there's a vibration approaching catastrophe

& I need to run away. I'm thinking
of language like it's something delicate

I can hold in my hand.
I'm worried that all of this might break.

Early morning & I don't care that it's starless.
It's okay that it's endless but full

of endings. It's November 15th & I'm left
without my normal faith in talk,

that I could fill a room with my voice
to tip the scales. Early morning

& sun gathers slowly in the clouds.
November 15th.

I'm Nate Pritts right now more than ever.
The trees are already empty. It's not fall

in Syracuse. It's fell.
It's exquisitely sinister. It's really this terrible.

I'm trying to be calm with the bomb in my hand.
I pretend I don't hear it counting down.

NOT BLOCKING THE EXPLODING

Tuesday clouds this hectic splatter, distorts
the calendar's faith in progression, its suspicion

of narrative. There's just this one next thing
plunked down, weighty & here, after the last

next thing burned off in mist. I say your name
out loud in the blue, in a field of fields,

in my own voice. I keep going. I teach myself
to control the forward fall. Sometimes

there's a breath in the trees that crowd the lakeshore
& sunlight pours through the canopy,

those brittle leaves not blocking the exploding light.
Sometimes writing this poem means I'm losing

some other one. I file a letter of acceptance.
Before clouds, a sun & from that sun

the dawn spilled everywhere & my backyard
could not contain it just as I could not contain

my backyard just as I could not contain that bird

& that bird could not contain me.

I would crush that bird if I could, pluck it
right out of the sky's big azure eye & squeeze

until it was nothing but history in my hands.
All day I've been watching these trees, waiting.

BRIGHT BRIGHT LIGHTS

This box will include more parts
than you know what to do with

& the architects will work hard
to make some new pain out of the old

Robots want to believe in their bodies,
that they can love but they can't.

All that metal hitting metal makes a noise
I can't stand   but I know that if I could see

the collision as it happens I'd tolerate it better.
They look at the sky & spit back a number

instead of falling into separate sad pieces.
For every blade of grass, they give you a chart.

There's not enough summer to let us forget.
            The stars are just whispers

that don't last   that don't last.

BLUEBIRD WHATEVER

Words only remind you about misery.
Your voice gets thick

with consequence early in the morning
before you even know all the wrong

that you'll say. Your brain is in shreds
but gets repaired by the clouds.
In place of the damage

is just static, just fluff.
There's a parking meter that wants

you to leave before you're done.
Maybe it has the right idea.
Maybe I need a trumpet

in my ear or a bash
to the jaw because I ruined the whole sky

with my thinking again. Here's another new life
you have to consider.
Wouldn't it be nice if the answers

descended among us?
Could whisper something earthly

though their skin is like sunlight?
The streets are a grid
which makes anyone feel perfect.

The breeze was so obvious
I had no choice but to feel it.

NEGOTIATION PROTOCOL

We will never give in to your demands.

But it's hard to say no   when the feeling
is moving   when the ocean is too simply
overwhelming.   We understand
that certain things are appealing

backyard gardens & pergolas
        wine   while everyone else is still working

because it signals that we're amazing
        that we're something different
something necessary that can't be ignored.

I've acquired a map
that dictates each of my next moves
        a launch to the moon   the right ways
to be desperate.

I already know how each strand of your hair will look
        in every possible circumstance
morning bedroom   each trajectory of wind.

Everything hurts if you do it right.

HOW TO SAY GOODBYE
EARLY MORNING

When the words don't add up, skyrocket
the picture you've kept
locked in your heart. If accumulation doesn't
make a poem, it might just be some drift. I'm just
snow; I'm typing miles of slush.
Today is decommission day,
a frantic blocked transmission
hitting its beak against the glass, lonely
for the living room. I'm done with
hummingbird. I'm ready to stay put or drop
broken to the ground after one frantic rush
too many. Some invisible
brick, some crack on the wing. I'm done
with trudge though I'm marshaling
my forces. I'm putting on my boots.
I'm going through maneuvers.
I can't remember if I mentioned the sun.
I'm afraid to look back & check.
I'm afraid to stop. The workings
a mystery; people, here are the results.
Here's the arc up my sleeve, ready
to throw down at the right time.
Here's the right time.
Here's the trajectory for today.
I'm gone.

DUMB WINTER

Drove through a hailstorm.

Got to appreciate the calm
        on either side of my day
the broad & blue sky
        a few clouds I could name.
Overhead there's one of those planes
flying so far away it looks bright
white
        like a young crab on the beach
translucent. Today I read
a few dozen lines from Milton
& Matt sent a new poem
which was terrific & quiet.
I can't tell if the birds are back
already or if they never left.
What an odd season.
                    What a dumb
winter. I haven't had a dream
that I remember in a handful of days.
I try not to think about
the money I owe, the letters I owe
to each of my friends.

I worry for a few seconds about nothing.

ICICLES GLINTING IN SUNLIGHT

Such impossible instructions! But our bodies try harder,
hollow & shivering. There are three states

blocking this me from that one – sparkly solid in near winter,
O impenetrable ineffable bloom! My fiery face melting

magma tears from the volcanoes chorusing, glacial
mist in this tectonic shifting. This continental drift.

The landscape will change. I know it will.
There's a dream to believe in about not falling down.

I can hold comets in my hand, grab each star out of
your eyes & make new pictures by connecting

those SOS dots & dashes, but the only thing
I can't do is something I haven't done.

Push for one last mile. Don't let the sun pass through.
Hold that light. Hold that light & today I can

fly from November to the heart of winter.
I'm clear empty & dripping. I wish I could feel more

better. I want to November it up. I want to

season the seasons. I want to fall harder.

I want to hang from the rooftops or dangle
from the bumper when you back out of the driveway

& head straight into beatitude. The brightest
words I can think of are grey & lonely.

That reverberating racket, belligerent & battering.
Icicles glinting in sunlight.

FEELINGS, ASSOCIATED

Tell me what I'm singing, lonely on the road buffered
with slush; tell me where I'm going when I rocket

this Syracuse into shimmering Poem, when I bracket
your You with my Me, take in the Cincinnati

with a big heaving breath. I'm mouthing barks
& yelps to the scatterment, risking this Pritts I've got

clenched in my fist & the Hart that you puncture
to spill out the fracture. You can't stop this

because it's the signal. This is the single, the lead off
stutter or the blistering fade, hidden track

to streak my broken interior when I inject the clouds
that stopped caring about me, where the weather

infests me. It's cold in this chest. It's my soul in the air.
Icicles glinting all around. The maddest mad scientist

& an honorary astronaut don't know what the fuck
they're doing but they're doing it again & again. Amen.

Pour the colored chemicals in a vat & see what blows.
Chart the dark from one galactic suicide to the next.

What are these words worth? Who else would believe
these trees & this sun & this Aeolian gust? Amen again.

I drive my sorry car, kiss the flagging moments as they go.
Leaping joyous over the fence & trampling the fields.

Put on a Coleridge face & bury your branches.
There's comfort in the tension of wood underground

breaking through, hibiscus & also the dirt not
blotting the hibiscus vesuvius. There's something bursting;

there's a bird listening. That's why I'm listing
some of the differences, & all that sameness, trash heap

mathematics to enumerate the particles, genuflect
to the rubble & honor the happy season we stopped

asking for reasons & listened to the feelings.

STARRY CONFIGURATIONS

Since every day could be
the very last day I see you, I'm
memorizing the blue of the sky

so I know what I'll have left
that I'm going to need

to forget. Sun bright snow.
January. Breath shattering.
I've got one pocket jammed full

of stones to keep me grounded.
Ballast so I'm uncleared

for blast-off. Too heavy for lift
off. Thwarted buoyancy so
I'd like to get out & look around.

Every day could be the last time
I have to watch you walk away

because you'll stay or just keep
going. But the trees have long since
dropped their leaves &, O, it's cold

in this goddamn town. I won't sleep

in your bed tonight. Watching

the sky for the terror lights.
Blinking silent slush from my eyes.
Something heading this way

& it's full of dismantling. Something
falling apart around me & it's

me or some starry conflagration.
Who ever said these points shining
made an image we could share?

Every day could be the day this sphere
drops behind the sun & every radio station

blares a reminder of that day I really loved.
Thank God for the static.
Thank God I can't hear it.

NEW COLOR OF THE BACKGROUND

Outside the window, a series of buildings
planted in snow. Snow blind in morning,

I'm relying on memory. Faltering
in restlessness, I'm feeling my way.

In the foreground, fake flowers, a sad blue frenzy.
Every day I can count on seeing some birds

& every day what the hell are they still doing here.
All these trees without leaves. Icy shatterings.

It's February in Syracuse. It's Syracuse,
New York in my heart & I don't know

how I got here. Except that I do.
Except I was gagged & blunted for years.

The map that I followed ran jagged & red.
You hold something close for long enough

& even sharp things blur. Gigantic,
but who can say what it was. Things in distance

look faded & smudged. They named this
perspective. They say that this blue looks bluer

depending. These shocks more shocking
because of old tremors & shakes.

Orange sunlight even in winter. You can idle
in a car & watch snow turn purple.

Your limbs heat up. Your body become bodied,
your breath & her breath. Now things are clear.

Remember all those parts you forgot.
The shade pulled low keeps out the night.

THINK BRIGHT

I walk into the fog & fall all apart.
The ghosts of some kids are flying around

through the trees, over the gravel.
Or maybe they're real – the kids I mean –

drifting in the air like moments
that already happened. I spend part of my day

sketching boulders & rocks, some scattered
all over & some stacked on purpose

by people who died, people who aren't
even people right now. All my poems

are captivity narratives where I play every part:
the abducted princess, the demon, the mountain,

even the clouds in the sky around them.
Sometimes I get killed but sometimes

just my identity gets ripped out from under me.
All the things that I did. Whatever

my dreams were. That's another new world
I won't have to remember. In this world,

I don't sleep easily. I'm living up in the air,
with the gods in the fog. Normally I live

under the sea with the fish people
& my secret horde of memory crystals.

You can scan them to learn everything about me.
For example, this white one is blank.

This yellow one too, so full of nothing.
An invisible narrative under constant pressure.

Whenever I close my eyes, the world goes away.

WAR MUSIC

It's warm for January   the end of the month
      a winter mostly without snow

& I am driving to get a coffee
      because without Jenny   my whole life falls apart

which is a privilege   since I am not worrying
      about getting bombed or shot

or debris falling from somewhere to crush my family
      I have an inner life   yes
          I spend so much time quiet

& when I say that my life falls apart   I only mean
      that I don't know how much coffee to make today

so I have to drive in my car
      listen to Haydn on the radio
      use money to buy whatever I want

& I haven't even done the dishes

from last night   have forgotten how
      to organize my time   which I take for granted

that instead of spending the day hiding & terrified

or getting shot in the face
         I know I will have this same face

tomorrow   & the same soft American heart
      my stupid American ego   I will not be dead

      my family won't be threatened
though we are already scattered & lost to each other forever

& right now I am telling my electronic friends about a muffin
      I will eat   it is so huge & absurd

& I am proud to have it
because I am huge   & dumb

I need to forget

because there is so much information
        I do not want to think about

because even here I will die   I will die quietly.

I AM WAITING FOR A GRAND GESTURE

I am driving my car through the snow,
each new collision a tiny patch
of numb. I am stuffing all this deterioration

into my heart. I am wondering if keeping
these broken shards makes me tough.
I am living in the old town. I am crash

landed with no map & I am stranded
but there is a hill in the distance & beyond
the hill is maybe just more distance.

I would like you to tell me the coordinates.
I have seen the bizarre shapes of the clouds
but these colors are new to me. I wonder

if I am not where I was before. What if
we are not who we used to be before?
I am looking out my window at the snow

of now & I am remembering then.
There might have been snow. There might have been
a different me walking near a different you.

We might not have talked. Words were like

these snow flakes, hushed & melting.
I am waiting for a grand gesture. I am

waiting for something to sweep me off
my slush or I am waiting for something
that will allow me entrance to the cosmos.

What if the star we saw blinking in the night
was only a radio tower? A grocery store parking lot
streetlight above your car? What if dawn breaks

& the stars fade whether they are stars or not?
What if I was broken
in two so you could put me back together?

35ᵗʰ BIRTHDAY VORTEX SUTRA

You charming blockhead, you sweet, sick mess,
   you sorry excuse, you so happily met,
             you you,
             you correspondent I,
   Nate, Nathan, Nate;
in full sunlight, or the whispered
         glow, wherefore can I
       now stand silent by:
         here, now, 35 today, hoping to cease not until death,
which
(let's hope) is deep
  into some imaginary future where
           the colors of the day
        are coordinated
  to our hopes & dreams & their
fading. How do I
       start this frenetic reverie,
       this noisy noise,
        when I know the past has left me
here alone without any tree to sing to
or a girl to call mine own or a fast fast car
  to take me spinning down the coast, dizzy
         with love,
         dizzy with hope.
  Ah, there is a colossal heart
in your hands, there is a colossal

head in your heart,
there is life & that fading
sound. There is
an urge to do good or nothing;
there is a bench in my chest that I
could sit on watching sunrise
after sunrise
after sunrise,
that eternal source of light, that ever
dawning, that always bright, adding
lustre to the day.
Syracuse amen, Asheville amen,
Brockport & Louisiana amen:
covered in my own dust, my me, those old
whatevers, but it is now & I have been
wrong before & I am right now, I am
hello New York,
I am hello:
I am an open heart beating time,
I am my friends scattered so I say
Los Angeles amen, Cincinnati amen, Chicago amen.
I say Missouri & Tennessee & Florida & Michigan
amen; I say I have lived too many lives,
I have seen the moon yelling at me, pushing me.
I have forgotten, I have been forgotten;
I can't take much more

                regret.
        Say you have follow'd far,
when well begun:
                say you have done your damndest
                say you have busted your ass.
                And he that stays
is you, he that stands is you & all honor
to your name, Nate Pritts, 35, ceasing not,
    blundering stupid, wondrous strange,
                foolish
                & so what.
    I can see so much of me, can see
with the flame of what bright light
                that, O, if there be more of this here
                then alright, okay—
                lonely & torn up & screaming
for more, hallelujah, Happy Birthday, amen.

THE END WAS A TOTAL SURPRISE
TO ME

Today's newspaper names three sad puppets
who couldn't hold their stuffing in
as their plush & colorful bodies

ejected from a car in the shattered dark
distance. There was a stilly hush.
There were icicles glinting in sunlight

as the animating principle was sped.
I snored or growled during this opera,
was labeled rude by well-dressed

persons. I slumbered as the voices sang
pain in such gorgeous syllables.
But I refuse to be implicated in the droning.

I proclaim allegiance to this fragmentary
grenade smuggled in my chest.
The newspaper turns me into a lake,

two spillway devices implanted in my face
where the run-off water leaks
when it gets to be too much. In my dream,

the driveway was lined with tulips, flashlight

landing petals for a luminous aircraft.
In my life, it's cold & I wake up

without you. In my dream tonight,
I'll plant tulips inside your body, blow on them
gently until the fire takes root.

RIGHT NOW MORE
THAN EVER

Acknowledgments, Notes, Thanks

Thanks to the editors, staff & readers of the following journals where some of the poems included here first found homes:

The Apiary / Apt / Barrow Street / Black Warrior Review

B O D Y / Cerise Press / Cimarron Review / Coldfront

The Collagist / Crossthreads / Forklift, Ohio / Fou / ILK

LIT / MAKE / Many Mountains Moving / NOÖ Journal

Open Letters / Parthenon West Review / Redivider

Spinning Jenny / Toad / Trigger / TRSNFR / Tuesday Night

The Tusculum Review / Whiskey Island / Witness

"The End Was a Total Surprise to Me," "Feelings, Associated," "Icicles Glinting in Sunlight," "In Memory of My Feelings" & "Talking About Autumn Rain" were included in the chapbook *FEELINGS, Assoc.* (Hubcap Art, 2010).

"Calm Poem" appeared on the blog for the Downtown Writers' Center/YMCA in Syracuse, NY.

"Collected Recollections," "Inarticulate Bird," "Post Fallout Letter" & "Sentimental Spectacular" were included in the chapbook *Sentimental Spectacular* (Mondo Bummer Books, 2010).

Part of "Rise Time" was published in a pamphlet by InDigest.

"Talking About Autumn Rain" was featured on *Verse Daily*.

Thanks for support (general & specific), instruction (solicited & unbidden), titles (offered & pilfered), friendship (deserved & un—) & good old fashioned love: Eric Appleby, S.T. Coleridge, Darcie Dennigan, John Donne, Matt Dube, Dobby Gibson, Allen Ginsberg, Liz Green, Richard Hugo, Robert Krut, Clay Matthews, Gina Myers, Scott O'Connor, Frank O'Hara, Alexis Orgera, any Pritts anywhere, Blake Schwarzenbach, Walt Whitman, X

& to Jenny Fortin for every literal thing.

This book is for my brother, Matt Hart.

Nate Pritts is the author of five previous books of poetry, including *The Wonderfull Yeare* (Cooper Dillon Books, 2010) & *Sweet Nothing* (Lowbrow Press, 2011) as well as several chapbooks including *No Memorial* (Thrush Press). His reviews & essays can be found in *Rain Taxi, Poet's Market, The Boston Review* & *PopMatters*, among other places.

The founder & editor-in-chief of *H_NGM_N*, an online journal & small literary press, he lives in upstate New York.

www.ingramcontent.com/pod-product-compliance
Lightning Source LLC
La Vergne TN
LVHW091202080426
835509LV00006B/791